THE SHARD
THE OFFICIAL GUIDEBOOK

THE VIEW
FROM THE SHARD

THE SHARD
THE OFFICIAL GUIDEBOOK

Thames & Hudson

Contents

Villas, Brothels and Chaucer's Canterbury Pilgrims

It's hard to imagine the dynamic quarter of Southwark close to London Bridge station and The Shard as a suburb, but here was London's first suburb, inhabited from Roman times onwards. The Romans built the first London Bridge (of timber) in the 1st century AD, a little downstream of the existing bridge. Around its southern approaches a settlement grew up, with substantial houses for prosperous citizens, on one of the islands that rose out of what was then a low-lying marsh, a flood plain for the Thames. Remains of two of these villas have been uncovered on the site of The Shard.

Like the City of London, Southwark went into rapid decline with the end of the Roman Empire; there is some evidence that, like the City, it was sacked and burned by Queen Boudicca's rebel army. Under the Normans, both the City and Southwark grew rapidly. London Bridge was rebuilt in stone. An important monastery, St Mary Overie (its church later to become Southwark Cathedral) and the hospital of St Thomas were established here, and churches and great houses, foremost among them the palace of the Bishop of Winchester, were constructed. Southwark, an area far smaller than the modern borough, became, in effect, the City's backyard. The inns – around two dozen of them – along Borough High Street housed visitors who could

LEFT This Roman inscription, formerly attached to a temple, was uncovered at Tabard Square, Southwark, and is now in the Museum of London. It reflects the significance of the area in Roman times.

TOP RIGHT : Winchester House, the London residence of the Bishops of Winchester up to the 17th century, was by far the grandest of a series of large houses in the Bankside area.

RIGHT Southwark's brothels were notorious. They survived efforts to suppress them by successive Bishops of Winchester (as lords of the manor). The prostitutes were nicknamed 'Winchester geese'.

ABOVE Geoffrey Chaucer's pilgrims gathered at the Tabard inn on Borough High Street before setting out for Canterbury. A fanciful view of the City of London forms the background to this medieval illustration.

LEFT The end wall of the great hall, with its remarkable rose window, is all that survives of Winchester House, downgraded into tenements and almost entirely destroyed by a fire in 1814.

'… In Southwerk at the Tabard as I lay
Redy to wenden on my pilgrymage
To Canterbury with ful devout corage …'

Geoffrey Chaucer, *The Canterbury Tales*, General Prologue

BELOW Southwark Cathedral stands on a site where there has been a church since Saxon times. The present building, given cathedral status in 1905, was the church of the Augustinian priory of St Mary Overie, founded in the 12th century and dissolved in 1539.

not be accommodated across the river, including the pilgrims heading for Canterbury celebrated in Chaucer's *Canterbury Tales*, who set out from the Tabard inn. Along the river, Bankside was an area of less salubrious taverns and brothels, a haunt of the less than respectable. Southwark had its criminals – and no fewer than five jails, including the Clink, run by the Bishop of Winchester (on whose land many of the brothels stood) and the Marshalsea (still in operation in Charles Dickens's days as a depository for debtors). Southwark was equally a place where industries not welcome within the walls of the City – for example, leather production and brewing – flourished (and were to survive into the 20th century).

For centuries, the City sought to exercise control over this expanding suburb – its independence grated – and gradually it secured limited powers to tax the inhabitants and round up miscreants. But the 'Borough' (which was not to gain formal borough status for centuries) retained its distinctive character. It was a place that attracted incomers and immigrants from abroad, who could find work in an area free from the regulations imposed by the City and its livery companies. Medieval Southwark – still physically separate from neighbouring settlements such as Bermondsey and Rotherhithe – was, in places, squalid and lawless, but it was equally dynamic, enterprising and open to new ways of making a living. It has retained something of this character into the 21st century, which has seen it emerge as a hub of business, culture and tourism at the heart of a world city.

Beer, Bears and Shakespeare's Globe

Southwark is famous throughout the world as the site of Shakespeare's Globe theatre – a replica of which, close to the site of the original, opened in 1997. The Globe, first opened in 1599 (and closed by order of Parliament in 1642), was one of four theatres along Bankside. Actors, like prostitutes, were regarded as an undesirable element by the City authorities. It is certain that Shakespeare and other leading playwrights such as Ben Jonson and Christopher Marlowe frequented the area. Bear and bull baiting, 'a very rude, nasty pleasure' in the words of the diarist Samuel Pepys, were other popular local pursuits that

thrived into the 17th century. The inns along Borough High Street continued to prosper: the street was described as 'a continued ale house with not a shop to be seen'.

During the Reformation the priory of St Mary Overie was dissolved and its church renamed St Saviour. The priory's site was soon built over. The local population grew rapidly in the 16th century, doubling in 50 years, despite the ravages of plague. Huguenots, fleeing religious persecution in France, were among the new wave of immigrants. Not for the first (or last) time Southwark became a hotbed of new ideas, including religious radicalism. Puritanism

BELOW A view of the City, seen from Southwark, by an anonymous 17th-century Dutch artist. Some of the theatres of Bankside can be seen on the left, with the church of St Mary Overie close to old London Bridge.

LEFT AND ABOVE The Globe theatre, where many of Shakespeare's plays were premiered, opened in 1599 and was demolished in 1644. A replica of the theatre opened in 1997, close to the site of the original building.

'... Can this cockpit hold
The vasty fields of France? or may we cram
Within this wooden O the very casques
That did affright the air at Agincourt?'

Shakespeare's reference to the Globe theatre, from *Henry V*, Prologue

BELOW, LEFT William Shakespeare probably lived on Bankside for a time while actively involved with the Globe theatre, where he acted.

BELOW, RIGHT The Swan theatre, opened *c.* 1595, is depicted in a sketch of 1596 – the only contemporary view of an Elizabethan theatre interior.

flourished. From Southwark, many emigrants set out to found colonies in the New World. Among them was John Harvard, who settled near Boston in 1637 and was the founder of Harvard University.

As Britain's trading empire grew during the 17th and 18th centuries, the riverfront along the south bank of the Thames acquired wharves and warehouses. New turnpike roads and bridges made the area more accessible: Blackfriars Bridge opened in 1769. Industries

flourished and new housing, much of it jerry-built, grew up to accommodate the workers. Gradually, the old core of Southwark was linked to surrounding settlements, extending into what had been fields, by new streets of houses. The area generated fortunes for some developers and industrialists, but it also contained some of the poorest slums of Georgian London. The animated street life of the area is vividly depicted in the artist William Hogarth's engraving of Southwark Fair, an annual event that continued into the 1760s.

LEFT The George Inn, now owned by the National Trust, is the last survivor of the many inns that once lined Borough High Street. Its galleried exterior still overlooks a large yard, which would once have contained stabling for travellers' horses.

RIGHT Southwark Fair, which filled Borough High Street for a fortnight every September, was established in the reign of Edward IV. Depicted here in an engraving by William Hogarth, it was finally suppressed in 1762.

Poverty and Industry in the Age of Dickens

Victorian London was the largest city in the world, a densely inhabited metropolis and the centre of a global empire. Southwark, which had once contained Roman villas and medieval palaces, was no longer a fashionable area. It was dominated by industry and by the docks, with ships still crowding into the Pool of London, downstream from London Bridge. Its slums were notorious: the novelist Charles Dickens wrote of streets where 'every repulsive lineament of poverty, every loathsome indication of filth, rot and garbage' could be seen. Dickens knew Southwark well: his father was held for debt in the Marshalsea Prison (described in *Little Dorrit*) and the young Charles was forced to work for a time in a local blacking factory.

While comfortable suburbs developed on its fringes, Southwark became a grossly overcrowded quarter of working-class housing in the shadow of the factories and warehouses. It was a place of 'haddock smokers, bone boilers, horse slaughterers'.

This was, however, an era of dynamic change. The coming of the railways fuelled the growth of the suburbs and spelt the death knell for the old inns of Borough High Street, which had served those arriving in London by stage coach. (The George, now owned by the National Trust, is the only survivor; see page 9.) London's first railway, from Deptford to Bermondsey, opened in 1836 and was later extended to Greenwich and to a terminus at

> 'His Majesty's revenues are seldom collected in this happy valley; the rents are dubious; and the water communication is very frequently cut off.'

Charles Dickens describing Southwark in *The Pickwick Papers* (1836–7)

Borough High Street in the mid-19th century. The railway was extended from London Bridge to Cannon Street and Charing Cross in the 1860s. Some of the buildings seen here still survive.

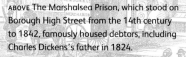

ABOVE The Marshalsea Prison, which stood on Borough High Street from the 14th century to 1842, famously housed debtors, including Charles Dickens's father in 1824.

London Bridge (built on the site of the old St Thomas's Hospital). This was to develop into the great transport hub adjacent to The Shard. At the end of the century, the Underground arrived in the form of the City and South London Railway (now the Northern line). The construction of Tower Bridge, opened in 1894, provided a new connection to the City.

With St Thomas's closed and relocated in Lambeth, Guy's Hospital (founded in 1721) became the most important centre of healthcare in the area. By the Victorian period, Guy's had developed a distinguished medical school. Poor housing and overcrowding provided a breeding-ground for cholera and typhus; life expectancy in mid-19th-century Southwark was just 35 years. Fire was another hazard: much of the warehouse area along Tooley Street was burned to the ground in 1861.

The Victorian age was one of steady social improvement. The building of Southwark Street (1864) cleared hundreds of sub-standard houses, but left several thousand people homeless. The social reformer Octavia Hill was a pioneer of improved housing for the poor of Southwark, while several new housing estates in the area were funded by the American banker George Peabody. Other philanthropists took an interest in popular education, but the breakthrough in providing a basic education for every child came with the establishment of the London School Board in 1870. Board schools became a feature of the landscape of London and paved the way for a better-educated, more democratic society.

TOP LEFT Charles Dickens knew Southwark well: he lodged in the area when his father was confined in the Marshalsea Prison in the 1820s. He recalled the old inns – 'great rambling, queer old places' – and set the first encounter of Mr Pickwick and Sam Weller in one of them.

TOP RIGHT An atmospheric view of Clink Wharf, Bankside, in the 1950s. The decline of the docks saw this area transformed, with many of the old warehouses demolished.

BOTTOM LEFT The great complex of warehouses at Shad Thames, Bermondsey, featured bridges spanning the narrow street. Many of these were retained as part of the late 20th-century project to convert the buildings into apartments, restaurants and shops.

BOTTOM RIGHT The rapid expansion of railway transport in Victorian Britain had a dramatic impact on the development of London. This ticket office in Borough High Street served the London and South Western Railway, which opened in 1838.

ABOVE Invitation to the opening of Tower Bridge on 30 June 1894. The bridge, with a lifting central section to allow ships to enter the Pool of London, provided a new connection between the City and the wharves and warehouses of Bermondsey.

Southwark Transformed in the Modern Age

'The ancient hospitality and freedom of the south are emerging once more in the twenty-first century'

Peter Ackroyd, *London: The Biography* (2000)

The historic heart of Southwark, close to the Thames, retained its Victorian character well into the 20th century, though slum clearance between the wars had removed some of the worst housing. Second World War bombs destroyed houses, factories and warehouses and provided a further impetus for rebuilding. Yet the essential character of the area, dominated by docks and traditional industries, did not change. The great transformation came with the decline of the capital's docks that began in the mid-1960s. The disappearance of Southwark's industries followed: tanneries, food factories and breweries closed, thousands of jobs were lost and Southwark (the modern, extended borough dates from 1965) faced an uncertain future, its population, for the first time in centuries, declining. Just across the river from the wealthy City, Southwark seemed very much the poor neighbour.

Moves in the 1960s to decentralize the London office market generated new office blocks close to London Bridge, but regeneration was the product less of new development than of the creative reuse of old buildings. Disused warehouses were converted into apartments. Hay's Dock was roofed over to create Hay's Galleria; in 1971, HMS *Belfast* was permanently moored near by and opened as a visitor attraction.

LEFT, TOP Tate Modern is one of the great art museums of the world, housed in the former Bankside power station and connected to the City by the Millennium Bridge.

LEFT, CENTRE Borough Market had its origins in a street market operating on Borough High Street, but relocated to its present site in the 19th century. In recent years it has become a major tourist attraction.

LEFT, BOTTOM Southwark, with its docks and industries, was a target for German bombers in the Second World War. The resulting devastation opened the way for post-war redevelopment.

RIGHT China Wharf, designed by the architect Piers Gough, was one of a number of new residential developments that began to transform the riverside in the 1980s.

FAR RIGHT Southwark Underground station is one of a series of architecturally striking stations on the Jubilee line extension, opened in 1999 and a major catalyst for regeneration in Southwark.

OPPOSITE The old divide between the City and Southwark has been broken down as new office developments such as More London, the site of London's City Hall, have transformed the south bank of the Thames.

Borough Market, close to Southwark Cathedral, a former street market that has operated on its present site since the mid-18th century, has become another major tourist magnet. A public walkway, where the rebuilt Globe theatre was a feature, opened up the riverside, which had been blocked off by wharves and warehouses. Bankside power station, widely seen as an eyesore when completed in the mid-1950s, was reborn in 2000 as Tate Modern, one of the world's great art museums, linked to the City by the new Millennium Bridge.

The regeneration process was boosted by improved communications. The London Underground's Jubilee line extension, opened in 2000, linked the West End with Greenwich and Stratford to the east and served London Bridge and new stations close by. A new Blackfriars station is under construction and the complete rebuilding of London Bridge station is imminent. Southwark is now a prime office location: London's City Hall is located alongside the river, as part of the More London development. The Shard, with its mix of uses and spectacular visitor facilities, is a powerful symbol of the continuing renewal of Southwark as, in the words of the writer Peter Ackroyd, 'one of the most vigorous and varied, not to say popular, centres of London life'.

'The Shard is a new London landmark, already a familiar part of the skyline. I want Londoners to be proud of it and have some sense of ownership.'

Irvine Sellar, Chairman, Sellar Property Group and Partner of LBQ Limited

BELOW The key people behind The Shard speak at a press conference to mark its inauguration on 5 July 2012: from left to right, Renzo Piano, Ali Shareef Al Emadi (Qatar National Bank), HE Sheikh Abdullah Bin Saoud Al-Thani (Qatar Central Bank) and Irvine Sellar.

RIGHT Irvine Sellar is Chairman of Sellar Property Group, the developer of The Shard on behalf of LBQ Limited. Joint owners of The Shard, LBQ Limited comprises the State of Qatar and Sellar Property Group. It is Sellar's vision and determination that transformed a dream into a building, creating what he sees as a vertical city district.

2. Meet the Developer

IRVINE SELLAR founded Sellar Property Group in 1991. With business experience extending over 40 years, Sellar has focused for most of that time on the commercial property market. Irvine Sellar originated the concept of The Shard and saw it to completion during a twelve-year journey.

Q: Where did the idea of The Shard originate?
IS: It was a matter of thinking outside the box. We'd bought Southwark Towers, a 1970s office complex, as an investment property. It made very poor use of a very good site. A government white paper was published promoting the idea of development around public transport hubs. We had London Bridge station next door, with mainline, Underground and bus stations: we made the connection! We had to work with Railtrack, succeeded by Network Rail – but they could see the potential for linking a development to major improvements to the station. So we tested the water, as it were, in 1999 with a proposal for a high building on the site, and got some positive publicity.

Q: But it was quite a struggle getting planning consent?
IS: I suppose that 9/11 made some people nervous about the project; we reduced the height of the building, which was originally planned to be 400 metres high. We finally got consent in November 2003, after fighting a public inquiry (we spent nine months preparing for it). CABE [the Commission for Architecture and the Built Environment, the government's adviser on architecture and urban design] had doubts about the project. English Heritage and Historic Royal Palaces opposed it. But we had

no problems with the community in Southwark or the local authority, and the Mayor of London was supportive from the start.

Q: How did you come to appoint Renzo Piano as architect?
IS: One of my colleagues knew and admired his work and suggested we talk to him. He had worked on projects around the world but wasn't known for designing tall buildings. However, he immediately saw the sense of a high-rise development at London Bridge. I remember meeting him in Berlin: he sketched his initial ideas for the building on a napkin over lunch in a restaurant. For him, The Shard was about rethinking the whole idea of tall buildings. I saw straight away that he was the man for the job. We appointed him in 2000 and the collaboration has been a spectacular success from day one.

Q: Was the idea of mixed use there from the start?
IS: The Shard is not so much a mixed-use building as a vertical slice of city, a place where people live, work, enjoy themselves. The 'roads' in this city are the building's banks of lifts and escalators. There is public access – highly unusual for a tall building in London, but something we thought was vital. The views are spectacular. The 'vertical city' idea was

one that Renzo found very appealing and his designs made it work.

Q: The Shard was controversial in terms of its impact on the London skyline. What do you think it contributes to London?
IS: The practical gains for Londoners are obvious. We've built a new concourse for London Bridge station, the fourth-busiest station in Britain, with 50 million passengers using it annually, with 75 million projected, and a new bus station. We're creating employment in Southwark. The Shard is a new London landmark, already a familiar part of the skyline. I want Londoners to be proud of it and have some sense of ownership. I can imagine the day coming when it's a listed building, part of the heritage of London, like St Paul's and the Tower.

Q. There is more to this development than just The Shard, though, isn't there?
IS: Absolutely. The Shard is just one piece of the wider London Bridge Quarter development, which is delivering a new district on the South Bank. London Bridge Quarter is emerging as a new social and commercial hub that combines The Shard, its sister building The Place, the transformed transport interchange, and new retail and public realm.

3. Meet the Architect

RENZO PIANO was born in the northern Italian city of Genoa in 1937, the son of a building contractor. Construction was in his blood. Over the last 40 years Piano has established a reputation as one of the most innovative of leading world architects. He first achieved international fame when, in 1971, with Richard Rogers, he won the commission to design the Centre Georges Pompidou in Paris. Opened in 1977, the Centre represented a revolutionary

Renzo Piano has been honoured with virtually every award the architectural world can offer.

approach to the design of cultural buildings. In 1981, Piano launched his practice, Renzo Piano Building Workshop (RPBW), which today employs around 150 people in offices in Genoa, Paris and New York. Piano has been honoured with virtually every award the architectural world can offer, including the Royal Gold Medal of the Royal Institute of British Architects.

Piano's work is notable for its diversity. He has worked on many arts projects, including extensions to major museums in Chicago, Boston, Houston, Texas and Atlanta. His Parco della Musica in Rome is one of the largest concert hall complexes in the world. As an urban planner, Piano has been responsible for projects at the Potsdamer Platz in Berlin and Central Saint Giles in London, as well as an ambitious regeneration of the old harbour in his native city of Genoa. Kansai, located on an island close to Osaka in Japan, remains one of the most radical airport projects yet realized.

A key theme of Piano's architecture is his interest in materials. His palette is broad. He used timber in a novel way at the Jean-Marie Tijbaou Cultural Centre in New Caledonia, rethought the idea of stone vaulting for the Padre Pio basilica in Puglia, southern Italy, and clad Aurora Place in Sydney, Australia, in translucent glass. It is a continuing interest in the potential of glass as a sustainable material that has driven the design of The Shard.

TOP ROW, FROM LEFT The Menil Collection, Houston; Jean-Marie Tijbaou Cultural Centre, Nouméa, New Caledonia; The New York Times Building, New York; Central Saint Giles, London.

BOTTOM ROW, FROM LEFT
Centre Georges Pompidou, Paris; Kansai International Airport Passenger Terminal Building, Japan; California Academy of Sciences, San Francisco; The Modern Wing, The Art Institute of Chicago; Isabella Stewart Gardner Museum, Boston.

1986

1977

1994

1998

2007

2010

2008

2009

2012

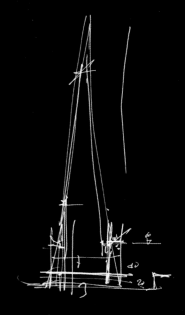

FAR LEFT Renzo Piano, architect of The Shard, is a prolific draughtsman, developing his ideas for new buildings in a series of sketches. These early sketches for The Shard bear a remarkable resemblance to the completed building and vividly express the key ideas behind the project.

Q: How did the project start?

RP: Twelve years ago, Irvine Sellar came to see me in Berlin. I'd never met him before, but he had the idea of developing a tall building at London Bridge. The Mayor of London was backing the idea. It was about intensifying the city, building in the heart of London, rather than encouraging suburban sprawl, creating a sustainable high-rise development on top of a major transport hub, served only by public transport, and with public access. Irvine's vision was immensely exciting. Some people thought it was impractical, even a little insane – but I've always sought to challenge accepted ways of doing things. So I agreed to become the architect of The Shard.

Q: One of the unusual features of The Shard is its mix of uses: offices, hotel, restaurants, apartments, shops, public space. Where did that idea come from?

RP: It was fundamental to the project from the start and something on which Irvine Sellar and I were in complete agreement, though many developers shy away from mixed use developments. I believe that successful cities have a 24-hour life – they don't close down when the office workers go home. I'm an Italian and 100% committed to living in the city. We've created the most public tall building in London, one that doesn't shut at 6 o'clock in the evening. It's a building that has changed the culture of development in London – just as the Pompidou Centre transformed thinking about museums. The Shard is a tall building with a difference, a new way of building in the city.

Q: You were fortunate, then, to have a client who was prepared to take risks?

RP: Irvine Sellar is a mould-breaker – he doesn't like doing the obvious. He fought hard to get The Shard built and convinced the Qataris to back it financially. For them it is a long-term investment – they are not interested in quick returns. We had to go through a public inquiry, which was tiring, irritating at times, but necessary; a project like this needs public support. The clients' support never wavered. I like to work with special people: you have to be able to say 'no' to some commissions. I don't run a huge office and have turned down many jobs. I'm lucky: I've never had a bad client. But in a project as large and prominent as The Shard, absolute trust between architect and client was vital, and that was what we had.

Q: Tall buildings remain controversial in London. How does The Shard respond to the character of London?

RP: Cities need new buildings as well as old ones. Again, I think back to Pompidou: we were accused by some of wanting to wreck Paris with an alien intrusion. Now the Centre is an accepted landmark. Wren's St Paul's was a radical intervention into the London skyline when new – and incidentally, I think it is a far finer building than St Peter's in Rome! Buildings have to express the spirit of change and inventiveness that drives great cities. Tall buildings, I believe, can enhance the city. They can be sustainable – and beautiful. The Shard couldn't have been built anywhere else but in London nor anywhere else in London except at London Bridge, close to the City, on a site where, we know, the Romans once built. It's a kaleidoscope that responds to changeable London weather, to light and shade. It's like a mirror, reflecting the city.

Q: So what's the secret behind designing a building as remarkable as The Shard?

RP: You have to have integrity, aesthetic as well as moral, and a total commitment to the poetry of construction. Sometimes you have to defend your vision against fierce opposition. Your designs have to be true to that vision, even if they are controversial. Sometimes controversy is necessary and inevitable. You have to be convinced in your own mind that what you are proposing is right – and then fight for it.

'The Shard couldn't have been built anywhere else but in London nor anywhere else in London except at London Bridge.'

Renzo Piano

4. Design of The Shard

Renzo Piano Building Workshop's designs for The Shard take their inspiration from London itself. RPBW is a practice with a deep concern for history and context and a long acquaintance with London. When developer Irvine Sellar first met Renzo Piano to discuss the possibility of his designing what was to be less a building, more a vertical city district, Piano made a series of small sketches that bear a remarkable resemblance to the completed building. He recalled historic images of masted sailing ships in London's docks and the varied steeples of Wren's City churches, just across the Thames from the site of The Shard. Equally fundamental to Piano's vision of the building was the idea of lightness and transparency. For all its height – this was to be the tallest building in western Europe – The Shard would be an ethereal presence on the London skyline, an elegant spire in contrast to the bulky high-rises of the past. Realizing this idea meant using glass in a highly innovative way.

RIGHT Renzo Piano's inspiration for the design of The Shard includes the shape of the ships' masts and church spires long associated with the city's skyline. They are clearly visible in the Museum of London's Rhinebeck Panorama, a striking watercolour of c. 1806–7.

RPBW worked with Irvine Sellar to develop the brief for the building, which evolved as a structure that could house the same mix of uses found in a typical central London street: offices, a hotel, restaurants and residential apartments. In addition, the building was to welcome the public: high up in the tower, a viewing gallery would offer spectacular views across London and beyond. Finally, the building was to be linked to London Bridge station and to the Underground, with a new bus station the final element in a heavily used public transport interchange.

The form of the building, as developed from Renzo Piano's initial sketches, reflected this mix of uses. The 24 storeys of offices, forming the lower section of the tower, make use of the large floor-plates on levels 4 to 28. Immediately above are three floors of bars and restaurants. The hotel would occupy the central section of the tower, with the residences above, where the building is slender enough for apartments to have views out on all four sides. The public viewing galleries were to be located at the top of the tower, with the spectacular glass-and-steel spire forming its summit.

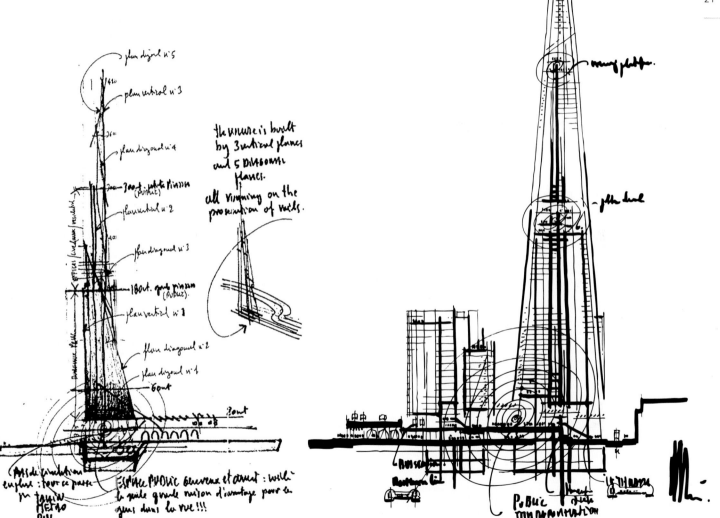

BELOW Early sketches by Renzo Piano demonstrate how the sources of masts and spires influenced the design of The Shard.

BELOW A more developed version of The Shard, showing how the ideas were transformed into a design for a building.

The Shard was to occupy a very tight site, occupied by 1970s office buildings (demolished as part of the project). The public transport links were a major driving factor for the development, but posed their own problems: a satisfactory connection to London Bridge station was vital, and work on the site, where deep piles would be needed to support the tower, could not disrupt the Northern and Jubilee lines of the Underground. The RPBW team worked with engineers and contractors to develop a strategy for building The Shard.

The Shard is dramatic in form, a new London landmark, but realizing the vision of the building as 'a shard of glass' meant getting the details right. Above all, the design of the façades was a critical issue, with large sheets of floor-to-ceiling glazing providing unobstructed views out. Clear glass, with a low iron content, was used, but the double-skin façade, equipped with blinds, makes for a building that is highly efficient in energy terms. Piano envisaged a building that would respond to the changeable English climate, to light and shade. The form of the tower itself is configured with views in mind, but equally to optimize climatic conditions for its users.

The mix of uses within The Shard meant that office workers, hotel guests and diners, residents of the apartments, and the public visiting the visitor galleries all had to have their own points of entry to the building, with no fewer than 44 lifts to whisk them to their required floors. In this way, the security, as well as the convenience, of all using the building is ensured.

LEFT A section through the London Bridge Quarter shows The Shard, with its connections to the mainline and Underground stations, with, to the left, The Place, a major office development also designed by the Renzo Piano Building Workshop. Across Borough High Street is Southwark Cathedral.

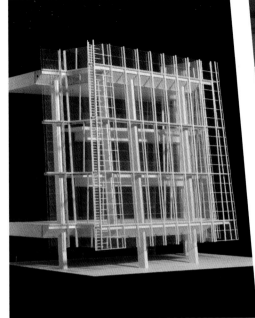

TOP LEFT The design of the glazed façades was developed using computer and physical modelling.

TOP MIDDLE/TOP RIGHT The floor-to-ceiling glazing offers unobstructed views by day and by night.

FAR LEFT Model of the new concourse for London Bridge station – a key element of the project.

LEFT The offices at all levels are finished to a high specification and offer fascinating views over London.

5. The Construction Story

The Shard took three years to build, with up to 1500 people working on its construction. Nothing about the project was simple: the team had to work on a constricted site, hemmed in by streets and buildings, including a major hospital, and overlapping one of London's busiest railway stations. Getting the building materials onto the site was a major exercise in planning. Those working there had to cope with a high water table, winds, heat and cold. The fact that the project ran to schedule was a result of a great deal of innovative thinking. Above all, the project was a triumph for teamwork, with everyone involved giving their very best to turning a vision into a building of which London could be proud.

1. Laying the Foundations

After the existing building on the site had been demolished, work began on putting in the foundations for The Shard, with 120 piles extending 54 metres (177 feet) deep into the ground [1, 2]. Each of these had to bear a weight of 2800 tonnes (3086 US tons) as the first 21 storeys of the tower were constructed around a central core. The Shard has three basement levels used for services and vehicle access, the lowest extending more than 13 metres (42 feet) below ground level [4]. Excavating the basements was a tricky operation, given the proximity of the Thames, so a massive retaining wall was built to enclose the site and provide a safe, dry base for the tower [3].

2. Getting the Right Mix

With the piling completed, the next step was to construct the massive concrete raft at the lowest basement level **[5]**. This provided the structural underpinning for construction of the upper floors of the building around the central core, which was being constructed simultaneously with the 'top down' formation of the basement levels. The construction of the 4-metre (13-foot) thick basement raft was an operation of heroic proportions: at the time it was the largest concrete pour ever carried out in Britain **[6, 7, 8]**. In a space of 36 hours, 700 truckloads of concrete were delivered, the trucks marshalled in a military-style operation.

3. Building the Core

The 'top down' strategy used to construct the basements allowed the concrete core of the building to be raised simultaneously [1, 2, 3]. A rig on top of the core was used to pour concrete as the structure rose. On top of the core a crane was installed, steadily rising as the core itself grew. Around the tower, four tower cranes were installed to deliver steelwork. In the final stages of construction, the site boasted the tallest tower crane in Europe. As the building rose upwards, conditions on site became ever more challenging, with work suspended on days when the tower was battered by high winds that made the upper levels potentially hazardous.

4. Floor by Floor

The Shard is essentially a steel-framed building constructed around a central concrete core. However, from level 41 upwards the frame is formed of post-tensioned concrete, switching back to steel for the 'spire' at the top of the tower. The lower floors were attached to the core, level by level, using fixings formed in the concrete **[4, 5]**, and by steel perimeter columns, the steelwork being craned up **[6, 7]**. Each floor has a metal deck, on top of which a concrete slab was laid. The concrete was pumped up from ground level so that work on the floors could continue even when high winds stopped the operation of the cranes. It was possible to complete a floor in a week, allowing the fast-track schedule of the project to be achieved.

5. Installing the Glazing

The Shard is clad with more than 11,000 individual glass panels, assembled in prefabricated sections to form a unitized façade system [4, 5]. These sections, assembled in a factory in Holland, incorporated two layers of glass, blinds and the motors powering them. On site, they were raised by lift and installed floor by floor; each panel typically took fifteen minutes to install [1, 2]. At the extremities of each floor, the glazing cantilevers out in tune with the idea of the 'shard of glass' [3]. Stainless-steel tubes attached to the façades support the cradles used for window-cleaning and maintenance.

6. Constructing the Spire

The strikingly modelled 'spire' forming the top storeys of The Shard contains some 1300 individual parts **[6, 7]** . Assembling it at the very summit of the tower was always a challenge: it could have been a question of learning in the sky. The decision was taken to assemble the structure in a dry run at the steel-fabricator's works in Yorkshire **[8, 9]**. It was then dismantled and transported to the site and assembled in sections. These were lifted into place and fixed into position with the aid of a team of expert steel erectors. With the installation of the final sheets of glass that give the tower its flamboyant crown, The Shard was complete **[10]**.

30

7. Fitting Out

The Shard contains a mix of uses – offices, hotel, restaurants, apartments and public viewing galleries – and the interior fit-out [1] reflects their different requirements. The offices are entered via a double-height lobby clad in white, hand-chiselled Carrara marble, giving the space a brilliant lightness [3, 4, 5]. In contrast, the visitor areas at the top of the tower are fitted out in dark wood, to minimize reflections and provide a warm and comfortable environment. On office floors of the building, a winter garden provides a temperate space, with fine views and the potential for opening windows to admit fresh air [2].

8. Creating a Transport Hub

A key driver of the project was government policy, which encouraged development close to major transport hubs. Serving 50 million travellers annually, London Bridge station falls into this category [6]. The Shard has delivered major improvements to public transport facilities, including a new bus station [7] and a new concourse, with a striking glazed roof to the train station [8]. The station is to be further redeveloped between 2012 and 2018, when its annual passenger count is likely to top 75 million. Two new pedestrian squares add to the quality of the public realm in the densely occupied London Bridge Quarter.

6. Inside The Shard

The tapering form of The Shard emerged in Renzo Piano's first sketches for the project. It is perfectly tuned to the mix of uses that the building contains: offices, hotel, restaurants and bars, the public galleries and residential apartments occupy the 72 habitable floors. The offices need deep floors. The hotel and restaurants require service areas as well as dining areas and guest rooms. At the top of the tower, the emphasis is on views on all sides, for the public and the residents in the apartments. The building is crowned by a dramatic steel-and-glass 'spire' extending up to level 95. At its base, The Shard connects to one of London's busiest public transport hubs, with mainline rail, Underground and bus services all enjoying improved access and better amenities for travellers as a spin-off from the London Bridge Quarter project.

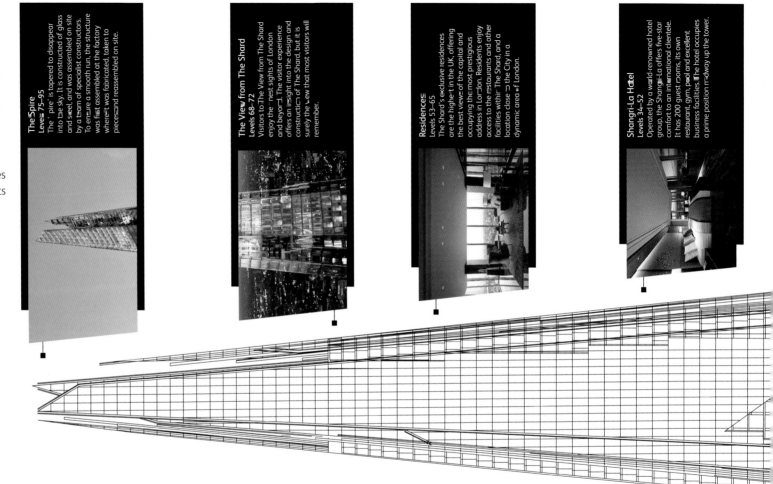

The Spire
Levels 75–95
The 'spire' is tapered to disappear into the sky. It is constructed of glass and steel, and was assembled on site by a team of specialist constructors. To ensure a smooth run, the structure was first assembled at the factory where it was fabricated, taken to pieces and reassembled on site.

The View from The Shard
Levels 68–72
Visitors to The View from The Shard enjoy the finest sights of London and beyond. The visitor experience offers an insight into the design and construction of The Shard, but it is surely the view that most visitors will remember.

Residences
Levels 53–65
The Shard's exclusive residences are the highest in the UK, offering the best views of the capital and occupying the most prestigious address in London. Residents enjoy access to the restaurants and other facilities within The Shard, and a location close to the City in a dynamic area of London.

Shangri-La Hotel
Levels 34–52
Operated by a world-renowned hotel group, the Shangri-La offers five-star comfort to an international clientele. It has 200 guest rooms, its own restaurant, gym, pool and excellent business facilities. The hotel occupies a prime position midway up the tower.

Level 95 Level 94 Level 93 Level 92 Level 91 Level 90 Level 89 Level 88 Level 87 Level 86 Level 85 Level 84 Level 83 Level 82 Level 81 Level 80 Level 79 Level 78 Level 77 Level 76 Level 75 Level 74 Level 73 Level 72 Level 71 Level 70 Level 69 Level 68 Level 67 Level 66 Level 65 Level 64 Level 63 Level 62 Level 61 Level 60 Level 59 Level 58 Level 57 Level 56 Level 55 Level 54 Level 53 Level 52 Level 51 Level 50 Level 49 Level 48 Level 47 Level 46 Level 45

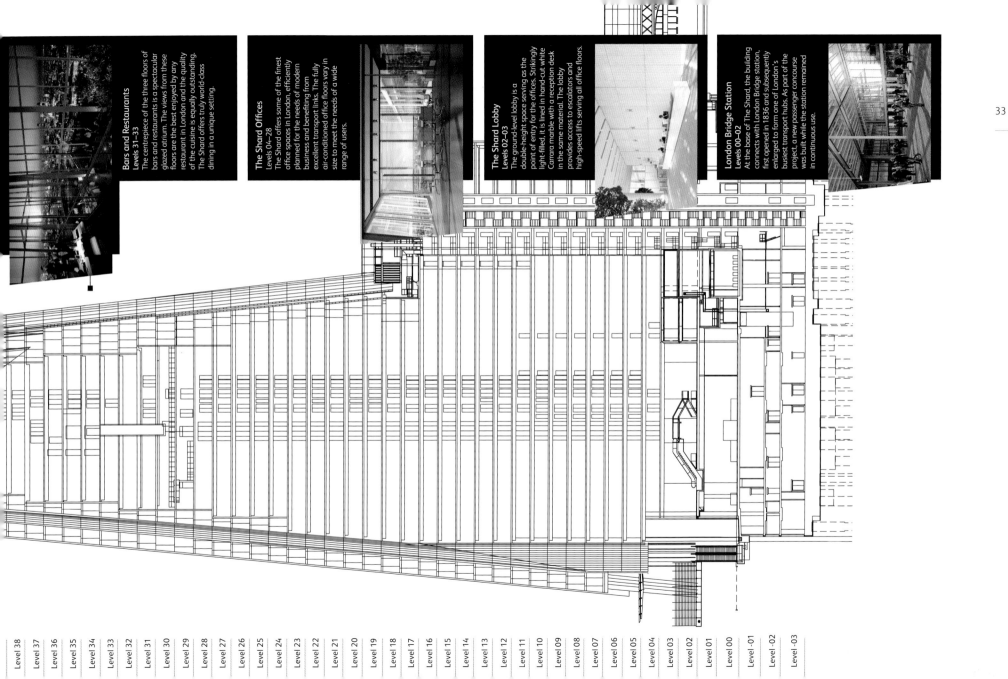

Bars and Restaurants
Levels 31–33
The centrepiece of the three floors of bars and restaurants is a spectacular glazed atrium. The views from these floors are the best enjoyed by any restaurant in London and the quality of the cuisine is equally outstanding. The Shard offers truly world-class dining in a unique setting.

The Shard Offices
Levels 04–28
The Shard offers some of the finest office spaces in London, efficiently planned for the needs of modern business and benefiting from excellent transport links. The fully air-conditioned office floors vary in size to meet the needs of a wide range of users.

The Shard Lobby
Levels 02–03
The ground-level lobby is a double-height space serving as the point of entry for the offices. Strikingly light-filled, it is lined in hand-cut white Carrara marble with a reception desk in the same material. The lobby provides access to escalators and high-speed lifts serving all office floors.

London Bridge Station
Levels 00–02
At the base of The Shard, the building connects with London Bridge station, first opened in 1836 and subsequently enlarged to form one of London's busiest transport hubs. As part of the project, a new passenger concourse was built while the station remained in continuous use.

Level 38
Level 37
Level 36
Level 35
Level 34
Level 33
Level 32
Level 31
Level 30
Level 29
Level 28
Level 27
Level 26
Level 25
Level 24
Level 23
Level 22
Level 21
Level 20
Level 19
Level 18
Level 17
Level 16
Level 15
Level 14
Level 13
Level 12
Level 11
Level 10
Level 09
Level 08
Level 07
Level 06
Level 05
Level 04
Level 03
Level 02
Level 01
Level 00
Level -01
Level -02
Level -03

7. The London Skyline

London's skyline has changed radically since the Second World War. Until 1939, the dome of Wren's St Paul's Cathedral was the tallest structure in the capital (at 111 metres/365 feet), the centrepiece of a panorama of spires and towers that gave the City its identity. Beyond the City, the clock tower of the Palace of Westminster – 'Big Ben' – was a prominent landmark (at 96 metres/316 feet). The reconstruction of London that began in the late 1950s generated buildings that overtopped these historic structures – Centre Point, the BT Tower, Millbank Tower, Knightsbridge Barracks, the London Hilton and Tower 42 (for a time London's tallest building). The tower of Guy's Hospital, close to The Shard, was a high-rise addition to the townscape of historic Southwark. In the 1980s the centre of attention moved to the Docklands, where Canary Wharf has grown as a major business centre with a cluster of towers, foremost among them One Canada Square. Until The Shard was completed, this building, opened in 1991, was the tallest in Britain (at 235 metres/771 feet). More recently, the City of London has become the site for a new generation of tall buildings, including the Heron Tower, 30 St Mary Axe (popularly known as the 'Gherkin'), and the Leadenhall Building (popularly known as the 'Cheesegrater'), the last designed by Renzo Piano's former partner Richard Rogers. But The Shard has no competition when it comes to height – or elegance. London is a world city and has a world-beating structure as a new symbol of its identity.

The White Tower – 1098
27 m/90 ft
Tallest structure in London
1098–1310

Nelson's Column – 1843
52 m/169 ft

Tower Bridge – 1894
65 m/213 ft

**Big Ben
Clocktower – 1858**
96 m/316 ft

St Paul's Cathedral – 1710
111 m/365 ft
Tallest structure in London
1710–1939

London Eye – 2000
135 m/443 ft
Tallest Ferris wheel in the world until 2006

BT Tower – 1962
177 m/581 ft
Tallest building completed in London in the 1960s

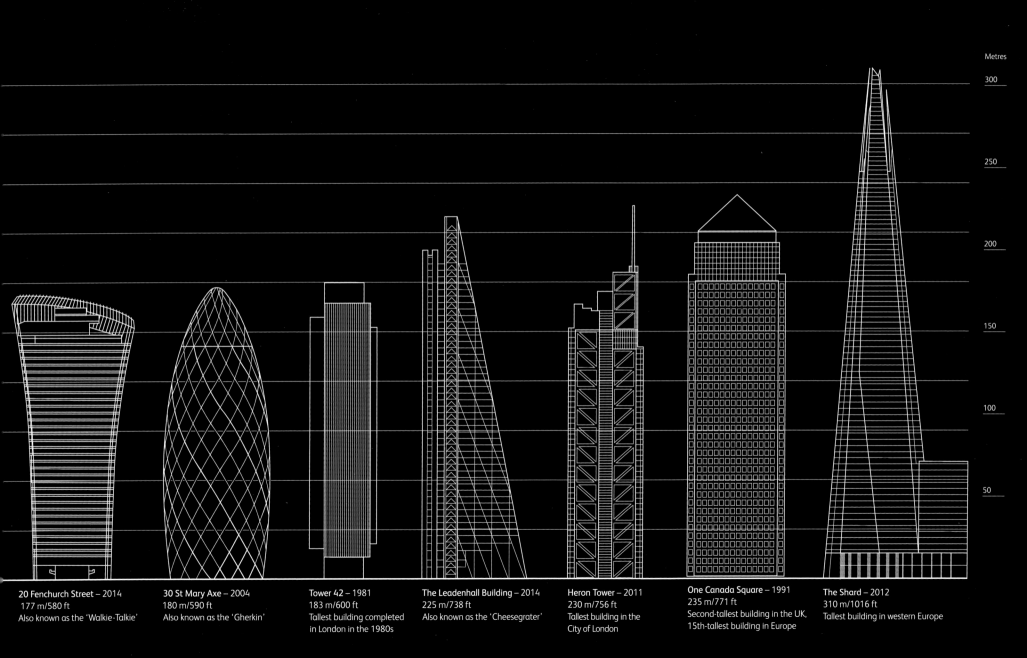

Metres

300

250

200

150

100

50

20 Fenchurch Street – 2014
177 m/580 ft
Also known as the 'Walkie-Talkie'

30 St Mary Axe – 2004
180 m/590 ft
Also known as the 'Gherkin'

Tower 42 – 1981
183 m/600 ft
Tallest building completed
in London in the 1980s

The Leadenhall Building – 2014
225 m/738 ft
Also known as the 'Cheesegrater'

Heron Tower – 2011
230 m/756 ft
Tallest building in the
City of London

One Canada Square – 1991
235 m/771 ft
Second-tallest building in the UK,
15th-tallest building in Europe

The Shard – 2012
310 m/1016 ft
Tallest building in western Europe

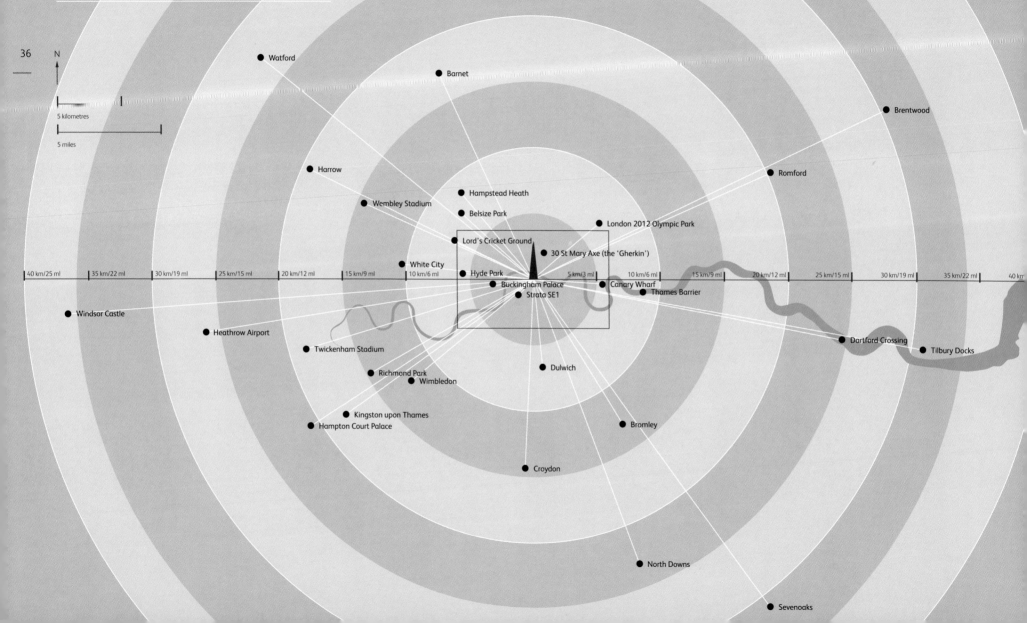

N

5 kilometres

5 miles

Watford

Barnet

Brentwood

Harrow

Romford

Hampstead Heath

Wembley Stadium

Belsize Park

London 2012 Olympic Park

Lord's Cricket Ground

30 St Mary Axe (the 'Gherkin')

White City

| 40 km/25 ml | 35 km/22 ml | 30 km/19 ml | 25 km/15 ml | 20 km/12 ml | 15 km/9 ml | 10 km/6 ml | 5 km/3 ml | 10 km/6 ml | 15 km/9 ml | 20 km/12 ml | 25 km/15 ml | 30 km/19 ml | 35 km/22 ml | 40 km |

Hyde Park

Buckingham Palace

Canary Wharf

Strata SE1

Thames Barrier

Windsor Castle

Heathrow Airport

Dartford Crossing

Tilbury Docks

Twickenham Stadium

Dulwich

Richmond Park

Wimbledon

Bromley

Kingston upon Thames

Hampton Court Palace

Croydon

North Downs

Sevenoaks

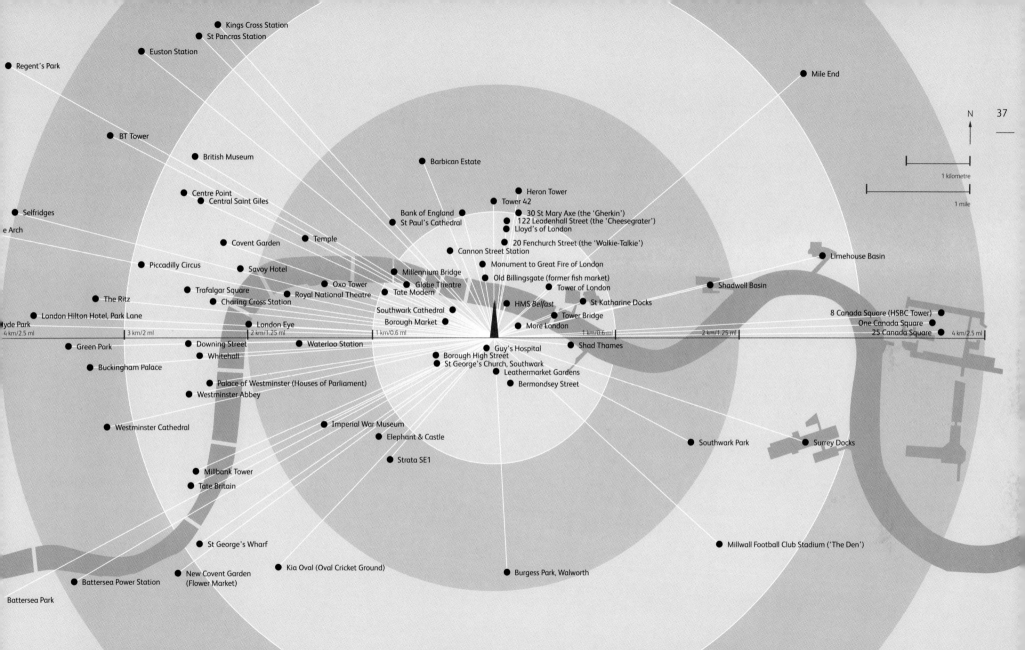

● Regent's Park

● Kings Cross Station
● St Pancras Station
● Euston Station

● Mile End

N

1 kilometre

● BT Tower

1 mile

● British Museum

● Barbican Estate

● Centre Point
● Central Saint Giles

● Heron Tower
● Tower 42

● Selfridges

Bank of England ●
● St Paul's Cathedral

● 30 St Mary Axe (the 'Gherkin')
● 122 Leadenhall Street (the 'Cheesegrater')
● Lloyd's of London

e Arch

● Covent Garden   ● Temple

● 20 Fenchurch Street (the 'Walkie-Talkie')

● Piccadilly Circus   ● Savoy Hotel

● Cannon Street Station

● Limehouse Basin

● Oxo Tower
Trafalgar Square ●
● Charing Cross Station

● Millennium Bridge
● Globe Theatre
● Tate Modern

● Monument to Great Fire of London
● Old Billingsgate (former fish market)

● Shadwell Basin

● The Ritz

● Royal National Theatre

● Tower of London

● London Hilton Hotel, Park Lane

Southwark Cathedral ●
Borough Market ●

HMS *Belfast* ●

● Tower Bridge
● St Katharine Docks

● 8 Canada Square (HSBC Tower)
● One Canada Square

yde Park

● London Eye

● More London

● 25 Canada Square

4 km/2.5 ml   3 km/2 ml   2 km/1.25 ml   1 km/0.6 ml   1 km/0.6 ml   2 km/1.25 ml   4 km/2.5 ml

● Green Park

● Downing Street   ● Waterloo Station

Guy's Hospital ●

● Shad Thames

● Whitehall

Borough High Street ●
St George's Church, Southwark ●

● Buckingham Palace

● Palace of Westminster (Houses of Parliament)

● Leathermarket Gardens

● Westminster Abbey

● Bermondsey Street

● Westminster Cathedral

● Imperial War Museum

● Elephant & Castle

● Southwark Park

● Surrey Docks

● Strata SE1

● Millbank Tower
● Tate Britain

● Millwall Football Club Stadium ('The Den')

● St George's Wharf

● Battersea Power Station

● New Covent Garden
(Flower Market)

● Kia Oval (Oval Cricket Ground)

● Burgess Park, Walworth

Battersea Park

122 Leadenhall Street (the 'Cheesegrater')
Rogers Stirk Harbour & Partners
2010–14

Barbican Estate
Chamberlin, Powell & Bon
1956–81

Lloyd's of London
Richard Rogers Partnership
1981–

Bank of England
Sir John Soane/Sir Herbert Baker
1790s/1939

Tower 42
Richard Seifert & Partners
1970–81

20 Fenchurch Street (the 'Walkie-Talkie')
Rafael Viñoly Architects
2009–14

Monument to Great Fire of London
Sir Christopher Wren and Robert Hooke
1671–7

N

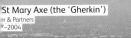

St Mary Axe (the 'Gherkin')
r & Partners
7–2004

London 2012 Olympic Park

Minster Court
GMW Partnership
1987–91

St Katharine Docks
1827–8
Redeveloped 1970s

Tower of London
Begun c. 1066

Custom House
David Laing 1812–17
Sir Robert Smirke 1825–8

Billingsgate (former fish market)
e Jones

One Canada Square
The second-tallest building in the UK, after The Shard
César Pelli & Associates, 1988–91

8 Canada Square (HSBC Tower)
Foster & Partners
1997–2002

25 Canada Square
César Pelli & Associates
1998–2001

St Katharine Docks
1827–8
Redeveloped 1970s

Tower Bridge
Horace Jones/John Wolfe Barry
1886–94

Tower of London
Begun c. 1066

City Hall
Foster & Partners
2002

HMS Belfast
1936–8

N

Thames Barrier
Second-largest moveable flood barrier in the world
1984

Millwall Football Club Stadium ('The Den')
1993

Shad Thames
See illustration, page 11

Railway to Kent
Including Canterbury and Dover

Millwall Football Club Stadium ('The Den')
1993

Railway to Kent
Including Canterbury and Dover

N

North Downs

Burgess Park, Walworth

Strata
Ham
200

N

Kia Oval (Oval Cricket Ground)
1868/2005

Elephant & Castle

Battersea Power Station
Sir Giles Gilbert Scott
1929–35, 1953–5

Battersea Park

Albert Bridge
1873

Imperial War Museum
1812–15

Westminster Cathedral
John Francis Bentley
1903

Palace of Westminster (Houses of Parliament)
Charles Barry
1840–70

Westminster Abbey
From 1245

Waterloo Station

St George's Church, Southwark
John Price
1734–6

Borough High Street

Battersea Power Station
Sir Giles Gilbert Scott
1929–35, 1953–5

Imperial War Museum
1812–15

Palace of Westminster (Houses of Parliament)
Charles Barry
1840–70

Westminster Abbey
From 1245

Buckingham Palace
John Nash and others
1825–1913

Waterloo Station

London Eye
Marks Barfield
1999–2000

St James's Park

London Hilton Hotel, Park Lane
Lewis Solomon, Kaye & Partners
1963

Royal National Theatre
Denys Lasden
1976

Hungerford Bridge
1864/2002

Waterloo Bridge
1945

Blue Fin Building
Allies & Morrison
2007

N

Wembley Stadium
Foster & Partners/HOK Sport
2007

Centre Point
Richard Seifert & Partners
1967

Central Saint Giles
Renzo Piano Building Workshop
2010

BT Tower
1964

British Museum
Sir Robert Smirke
1857

St Paul's Cathedral
Sir Christopher Wren
1669–1711

Tate Modern extension
Herzog & de Meuron
2013–16

Blackfriars Bridge
1860–69

Millennium Bridge
Foster & Partners/Ove Arup & Partners/Sir Anthony Caro
1996–2001

Tate Modern
Originally Bankside Power Station, Sir Giles Gilbert Scott, 1947–63
Refurbished by Herzog & de Meuron, 2000

Southwark Bridge
1912–21

Cannon Street Station

Cannon Street Railway Bridge
1863–6

Southwark Cathedral (just out of view)
Begun 12th century (given cathedral status 1905)

The Tower of London

The Tower of London was begun towards the end of 1066, soon after the Battle of Hastings secured the Norman conquest of England. The most prominent structure, the White Tower, was completed in 1078. The Tower of London has served a variety of functions: originally an important defence structure and royal palace, it has also been a prison and place of execution, an armoury, a treasury, a menagerie (the origins of London Zoo), the home of the Royal Mint, a public record office, and the home of the Crown Jewels. Today the Tower is one of Britain's most popular sites, attracting close to three million visitors a year.

HMS *Belfast*

HMS *Belfast* was constructed in its eponymous city and launched in 1938. It is a rare survival of a British World War II warship. In its day the largest and most powerful cruiser in the Royal Navy fleet, the vessel was involved in protecting the arctic convoys sending supplies to Russia, and served in the D-Day landings. Later, HMS *Belfast* played an active role in the Korean War from 1950 to 1952. The warship was retired from service in 1963 and since 1971 has been open to the public, under the curatorial care of the Imperial War Museum.

Tower Bridge

Tower Bridge, designed by Horace Jones, architect to the City of London, and the engineer John Wolfe Barry, opened in 1894. It is a reminder of the significance of London as a major port: its roadway is divided into two sections, each of which can be raised (originally using steam engines, which may still be seen today) to allow tall ships to pass under the bridge. The upper level, originally a pedestrian walkway that could be used when the bridge was raised, closed in 1910, but has since been opened to the public as part of the Tower Bridge Experience.

City Hall and More London

City Hall, the seat of the Greater London Authority and the Mayor of London, is a distinctive landmark on the South Bank. Opened in 2002, the building was designed by Foster & Partners: its centrepiece, the assembly chamber, is topped by a spiralling ramp, its form expressed externally. City Hall forms an integral part of the More London development, constructed on a long-derelict dockland site. With a series of office buildings, also designed by Foster, a hotel, and the Unicorn children's theatre (2005) designed by Keith Williams Architects, the project reflects the ongoing regeneration of Southwark.

Olympic Park

The Olympic Park was the principal venue of the London 2012 Olympic and Paralympic Games. The games were awarded to London in 2005, after which the site was extensively developed, giving new life to old industrial and railway lands. A team of architects was commissioned to create the principal stadium, an aquatic centre and velodrome, and an extensive village for the athletes. The tallest structure on the site is the ArcelorMittal Orbit, a sculpture and observation tower designed by artist Anish Kapoor with engineer Cecil Balmond. The site has been transformed into one of the largest new urban parks in Europe.

Canary Wharf

Canary Wharf has been developed on the site of former docklands to become one of the prime business locations in Europe. Initially viewed as competition by the City of London, the district today helps to confirm London's position as one of the world's foremost financial capitals. The tallest tower in Canary Wharf, One Canada Square, designed by César Pelli and completed in 1991, is the second-tallest building in Britain, after The Shard.

The View North West

The BT Tower (177 metres/581 feet) was the tallest building in London from its completion in 1964 until 1980, when its height was exceeded by Tower 42 (see page 34). The slim cylindrical structure had a technical function: to transmit telecommunications throughout Britain. In 1966 the revolving restaurant on the 34th floor opened to the public and remained in use until 1980. The brightly clad buildings to the left, a complex of shops, restaurants, offices and apartments known as Central Saint Giles, opened in 2010, and is the only other project in London by Renzo Piano, architect of The Shard.

Battersea Power Station

Battersea Power Station was constructed in two phases, in the 1930s and 1950s, to designs by the eminent architect Sir Giles Gilbert Scott. The structure remains the largest brick building in Europe, and originally supplied one-fifth of London's electricity, consuming one million tons of coal a year. The power station finally closed in 1983. After a variety of schemes to develop the site were abandoned, it is at last being redeveloped for housing, offices and other uses, with the original brick structure at its core.

Palace of Westminster

The Palace of Westminster (popularly known as the Houses of Parliament, and the seat of government in Great Britain, containing the House of Commons and the House of Lords) was designed in the 19th century in Gothic style by Sir Charles Barry and A.W.N. Pugin. It replaced the medieval palace that had largely been destroyed by fire in 1834. The only surviving part of the original building is the magnificent Westminster Hall. Norman in origin, the present hall was completed in 1401 and remains the largest space within the palace. Of the two main towers at the Palace of Westminster, the best known is commonly referred to as Big Ben, although that is properly the name only of the great bell of its famous clock.

London Eye

The London Eye (135 metres/443 feet tall), designed by architects Marks Barfield and opened in 2000, is the largest Ferris wheel in Europe. It contains 32 capsules, each accommodating up to 25 people, and revolves once every 30 minutes. It was the highest public viewing point in London until The View from The Shard opened in early 2013.

Millennium Bridge

The Millennium Bridge, designed by Foster & Partners with engineers Arup and sculptor Sir Anthony Caro, opened in 2000. The only bridge over the River Thames in central London designed solely for pedestrian use, it is a steel suspension bridge, 325 metres/1,066 feet long, and connects two of London' most popular visitor attractions, St Paul's Cathedral and Tate Modern.

Tate Modern

Tate Modern, one of the world's foremost museums of modern and contemporary international art, occupies the former Bankside Power Station, which was designed in the mid-20th century by Sir Giles Gilbert Scott, the architect of Battersea Power Station (see p. 51). The building was converted into a museum by Swiss architects Herzog & de Meuron and opened in 2000. The most striking internal feature is the vast turbine hall, which once housed the electricity generators. A new space for the museum, also designed by Herzog & de Meuron, is under construction on the south side of the site and is due to open in 2016.

Southwark Cathedral

Southwark Cathedral is one of London's most significant medieval survivals. Originally the church of the Augustinian Priory of St Mary Overie, founded in 1106 and dissolved by Henry VIII in 1539, it subsequently served as a parish church but became the mother church of the new Anglican diocese of Southwark in 1905. The nave is an addition of the 1890s, the original structure having been demolished in 1839. The new cloister was opened by Nelson Mandela in 2001.

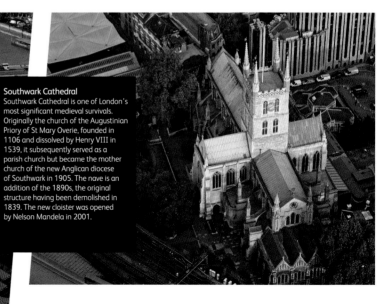

St Paul's Cathedral

St Paul's Cathedral is one of the prime landmarks of London and one of the best-known churches in the world, its great dome a symbol of the capital. (Until 1962 it was, at 111 metres/365 feet, the tallest structure in London.) The present cathedral was constructed between 1669 and 1710 to designs by Sir Christopher Wren, replacing its medieval predecessor, destroyed in the Great Fire of London of 1666. It is one of the finest examples of Baroque architecture in Britain. The cathedral has been the site of many state occasions, including the funerals of Lord Nelson and Winston Churchill and the wedding of the Prince of Wales and Princess Diana.

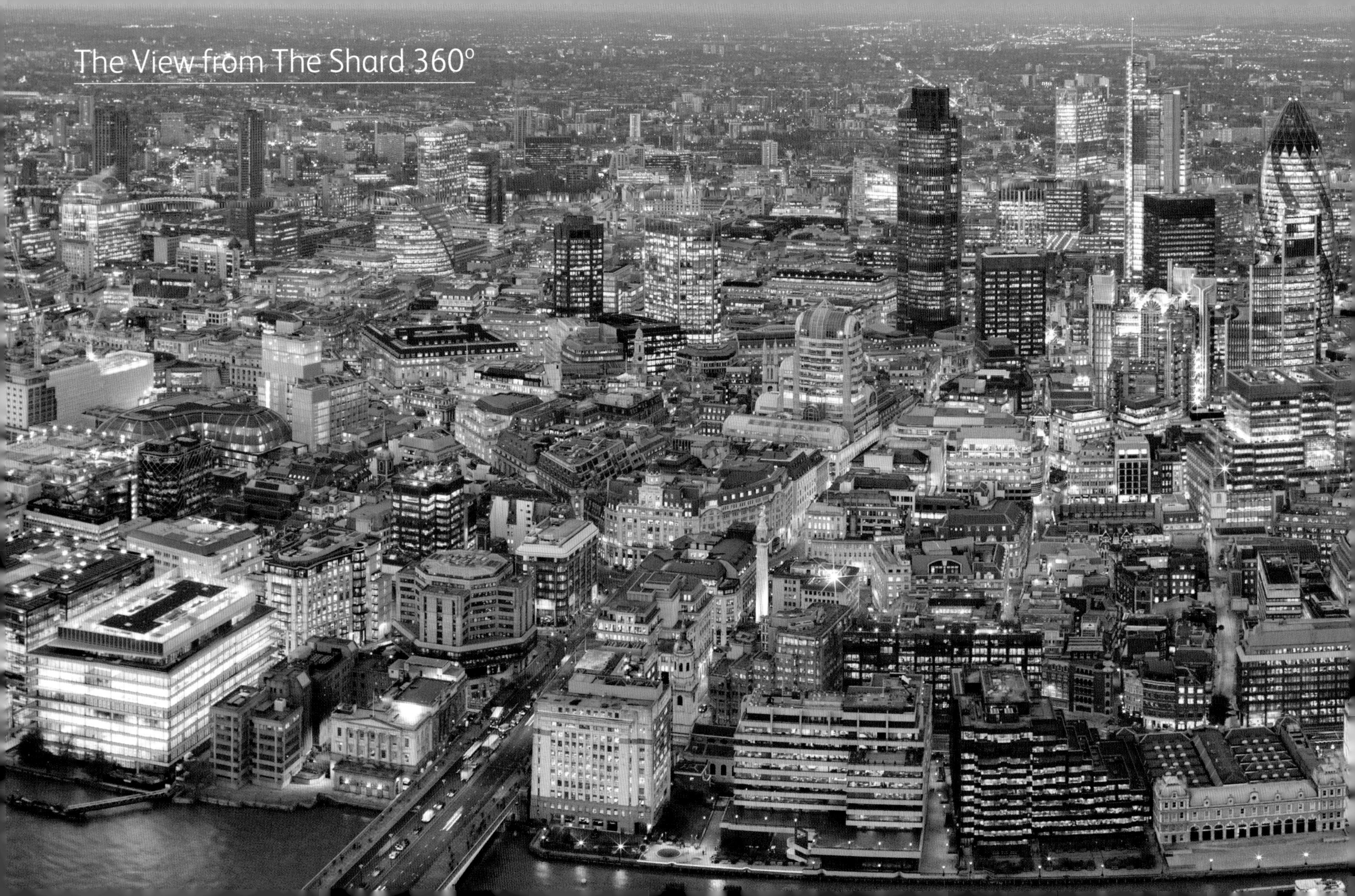

9. Fascinating Facts

Why is it called The Shard?
The name 'Shard' derives from the building's sculpted design, which consists of tapering glass facets that do not meet at the top. The summit therefore resembles jagged shards of glass, while the building as a whole is reminiscent of an inverted icicle.

How tall is The Shard?
The building, the tallest habitable structure in western Europe, rises to a height of almost a third of a kilometre: 309.6 metres, or 1,016 feet. Although 95 storeys high, the highest habitable floor is level 72, the upper viewing gallery, which is 244 metres (800 feet) high. The building is served by 44 lifts, some of which are double-decker.

How much material was used in The Shard's construction?
- Total volume of concrete: 54,000 m^3/1,907,000 ft^3 – equivalent to 22 Olympic-sized swimming pools
- Total volume of concrete in the central core: 18,440 m^3/651,200 ft^3
- Total volume of concrete in the foundations: 14,711 m^3/519,500 ft^3
- Glazing, by area: 56,000 m^2/602,800 ft^2 – almost two-and-a-half times the size of Trafalgar Square, or the equivalent to 8 football pitches
- Glazing, by number of individual panels: 11,000
- Total length of wiring: 320 km/200 miles – the distance from London to Paris
- Total length of pipework: 60 km/38 miles

How many people constructed The Shard?
During the peak construction phase, 1,450 construction workers were employed on site, representing 60 nationalities.

How far can one see from the viewing galleries on a clear day?
The upper viewing gallery, on level 72, offers views that, on a clear day, extend to approximately 55 km (35 miles) in each direction – from Heathrow to the west to the Thames estuary in the east. No other public viewing space in London offers views over such distances.

How does The Shard cope in high winds?
The Shard has a concrete core, around which a steel structure offers both stability and a highly engineered degree of flexibility in very high winds, when the tower has been designed to move by up to 50 cm (20 in). To prevent the building becoming an inverted pendulum in such conditions, movement at the top of the building is dampened using steel tendons that are kept taut with hydraulic jacks.

Is The Shard environmentally friendly?
Yes. The building is clad using triple-glazed units, the middle layer of which is designed to shield the interior of the building from excessive heat gain from the sun. The outer layer of glass, which contains low levels of iron (the ingredient that gives a lot of glass its green tint), is unusually clear, not only reflecting the sunlight and thereby minimizing the build-up of heat internally, but also making the building attractively transparent. The building is also naturally ventilated: small gaps between all the glazing panels are designed to allow a constant airflow.

How do they clean the windows?
The glazed façade incorporates a number of elements that operate like up-and-over garage doors. From these openings cradles are released, and are guided down the building on stainless-steel tubes to facilitate not only window cleaning, but also external maintenance. The uppermost windows are cleaned by abseilers – a job that requires a good head for heights.

Picture Credits

Acknowledgments

The author and publishers are particularly grateful to Renzo Piano, William Matthews and Stefania Canta of Renzo Piano Building Workshop (RPBW) for their generous help and advice during the production of this book. Special thanks are also owed to photographer Dennis Gilbert and to Charles Mavor, Anders Nyberg, Laura McCarthy, Lucy James, Lisa King, Joanne Davis and Charlotte Alldis for their kind assistance throughout the project.

The Shard is owned by LBQ Limited, comprising the State of Qatar (the majority shareholder) and Sellar Property Group, with non-equity funding from Qatar National Bank.

The State of Qatar has a strong commitment to invest and build in the UK as part of Qatar's 2030 Vision, which is the country's roadmap to achieving a sustainable, diversified economy, and The Shard forms part of this portfolio.

First published in the United Kingdom in 2013 by Thames & Hudson Ltd, 181A High Holborn, London WC1V 7QX

Second edition 2015

The Shard: The Official Guidebook © 2013 and 2015 Thames & Hudson Ltd, London
Text © 2013 and 2015 Thames & Hudson Ltd, London
Illustrations © 2013 and 2015 the copyright holders; see Picture Credits

Text: Kenneth Powell
Book design and layout: Peter Dawson, www.gradedesign.com
Pages 34–37: Illustrations copyright © Grade Design Consultants Ltd

Cover, front and back: Photos © Andy Stagg

British Library Cataloguing-in-Publication Data
A catalogue record for this book is available from the British Library

ISBN 978-0-500-34307-4

Printed and bound in China by Toppan Leefung Printing Limited

To find out about all our publications, please visit **www.thamesandhudson.com**. There you can subscribe to our e-newsletter, browse or download our current catalogue, and buy any titles that are in print.